Dear Parent:

Congratulations! Your child is taking the first steps on an exciting journey. The destination? Independent reading!

STEP INTO READING® will help your child get there. The program offers books at five levels that accompany children from their first attempts at reading to reading success. Each step includes fun stories, fiction and nonfiction, and colorful art. There are also Step into Reading Sticker Books, Step into Reading Math Readers, and Step into Reading Phonics Readers— a complete literacy program with something to interest every child.

Learning to Read, Step by Step!

Ready to Read   Preschool–Kindergarten
• big type and easy words • rhyme and rhythm • picture clues
For children who know the alphabet and are eager to begin reading.

Reading with Help   Preschool–Grade 1
• basic vocabulary • short sentences • simple stories
For children who recognize familiar words and sound out new words with help.

Reading on Your Own   Grades 1–3
• engaging characters • easy-to-follow plots • popular topics
For children who are ready to read on their own.

Reading Paragraphs   Grades 2–3
• challenging vocabulary • short paragraphs • exciting stories
For newly independent readers who read simple sentences with confidence.

Ready for Chapters   Grades 2–4
• chapters • longer paragraphs • full-color art
For children who want to take the plunge into chapter books but still like colorful pictures.

STEP INTO READING® is designed to give every child a successful reading experience. The grade levels are only guides. Children can progress through the steps at their own speed, developing confidence in their reading, no matter what their grade.

Remember, a lifetime love of reading starts with a single step!

For Ashley and Inha—S.C.

Text copyright © 2003 by Shana Corey. Illustrations copyright © 2003 by Dan Andreasen.
All rights reserved under International and Pan-American Copyright Conventions.
Published in the United States by Random House Children's Books, a division of Random House,
Inc., New York, and simultaneously in Canada by Random House of Canada Limited, Toronto.

www.stepintoreading.com

Educators and librarians, for a variety of teaching tools, visit us at
www.randomhouse.com/teachers

Library of Congress Cataloging-in-Publication Data
Corey, Shana.
Joan of Arc / by Shana Corey ; illustrated by Dan Andreasen.
p. cm. — (Step into reading. Step 4 book)
ISBN 0-375-80620-2 (trade) — ISBN 0-375-90620-7 (lib. bdg.)
1. Joan, of Arc, Saint, 1412–1431—Juvenile literature. 2. France—History—Charles VII, 1422–1461—
Juvenile literature. 3. Christian saints—France—Biography—Juvenile literature. [1. Joan, of Arc,
Saint, 1412–1431. 2. Saints. 3. Women—Biography. 4. France—History—Charles VII, 1422–1461.]
I. Andreasen, Dan, ill. II. Title. III. Series.
DC103.5 .C67 2003
944'.026'092—dc21 [B] 2001019625

Printed in the United States of America First Edition 10 9 8 7 6 5 4 3 2 1

STEP INTO READING, RANDOM HOUSE, and the Random House colophon are registered trademarks
of Random House, Inc.

Joan of Arc

by Shana Corey

illustrated by Dan Andreasen

Random House 🏠 New York

Joan of Arc was ready for battle. Her hair was cut as short as a boy's. She wore a suit of armor made just for her. She had a white banner blazing with gold lilies.

There was only one thing missing— a sword.

Joan had seen the sword she wanted in a vision. It was an old sword, hidden in a nearby church.

Joan sent a messenger to the church to look for it. Just as Joan had said, he found an old box behind the altar. Inside, there was a sword covered with rust.

April 2, 1429, Sainte-Catherine-de-Fierbois

When the sword was cleaned, the rust
fell away. The blade sparkled in the
sunlight.

The messenger raced back to Joan and
gave her the sword. She held it high. She
knew it would bring France victory.

When the time came, Joan jumped onto her horse and charged into battle.

May 4, 1429, Orléans

The French army saw the flash of her sword. Her bravery gave them the strength they needed. The French triumphed!

Seventeen-year-old Joan of Arc had won her first battle.

Joan of Arc was not always a famous leader.

France had been at war with England since 1337, long before Joan was born. Some of the French people supported the English. They were called Burgundians (bur-GUN-dee-unz) after their leader, the Duke of Burgundy. They fought over who would rule France.

When Joan was born in 1412, the French, the English, and the Burgundians had been fighting for almost a hundred years!

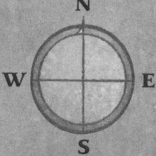

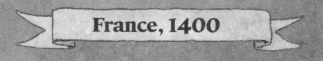

France, 1400

Joan grew up on a small farm in France, in the district of Lorraine (luh-RANE). She did not go to school. And she never learned to read or write.

Instead, Joan took care of the cows and sheep. She planted vegetables. And she helped her mother spin wool into yarn. While they worked, Joan's mother told her stories about saints.

When Joan was not working, she went to church or played with her friends. She was just a normal girl living in the 1400s.

But Joan would not be a normal girl for long.

One day, something happened that changed Joan's life—and history—forever.

She was in the garden. Suddenly, she saw a bright light. Then she heard voices!

At first, Joan was afraid. But the voices were kind and gentle. They told her that she had been chosen to save France. Joan thought the voices were sent by God.

She made up her mind to do what the voices told her. She made up her mind to save France.

French legend said that a girl from Lorraine would be the one to stop the fighting and save the country.

Could Joan be that girl?

Circa 1425, village of Domrémy, Lorraine

The voices said she was.

After that first day in the garden, the voices came back to Joan again and again. They told her that she would drive out the English and get the French Prince, Charles the Seventh, crowned King.

Joan did not tell her parents about the voices or about her dangerous mission. But her father had a dream that Joan dressed in boys' clothes and went to war.

Finally, the voices told her it was time to begin. With her parents' permission, Joan went to visit her cousins. They lived near an army camp.

Joan had a meeting with the army's commander. She told him she was going to save France. She asked him to help her see the Prince.

The commander laughed. How could a young girl save a country when grown men had been trying for almost a hundred years? He sent Joan away.

May 13, 1428, Vaucouleurs

Things got worse for France. The city of Orléans (or-lay-AHN) was surrounded by the English. Its people were starving. They could not hold out much longer.

On her seventeenth birthday, Joan went to see the commander again.

The commander was willing to try anything now. He agreed to help Joan.

He gave her a horse and a suit of armor. He asked a group of guards to escort her to the town of Chinon (shee-NOAN), where the Prince was staying.

Traveling was dangerous. So Joan cut her hair like a boy's. She dressed in boys' clothes under her armor. Her journey would be safer that way.

February 2, 1429, Vaucouleurs

February 23, 1429, en route to Chinon

Word spread about the girl who said
she could bring peace. When Joan left
Vaucouleurs (voh-koo-LUHR), the entire
town came to watch. For better or worse,
Joan was on her way.

Joan and her guards rode across
France. The guards were practiced
horsemen. They were surprised that Joan
could keep up with them. But she did.

"Faster! Faster!" she cried when they
slowed down. "We must hurry!"

News about Joan and her voices had
already reached the Prince. When she
arrived, he wanted to see if she really
did have special powers.

Joan came to meet him in the Great
Hall of the castle where he was living.
But the Prince was not on his throne.

Instead, the room was filled with
people. Anyone could have been the
Prince.

But Joan went straight to the real Prince and bowed.

"*I* am not the King!" he said with a laugh.

Joan shook her head. "It is you and none other," she told him.

Everyone was amazed!

Joan told the Prince she would free the city of Orléans. Then, she said, she would see him crowned King of France. Joan asked him to send her into battle soon.

"I shall last but one year, or maybe a little over," she warned him.

March 6, 1429, Chinon

The Prince believed Joan. But he did not send her to Orléans right away.

In the 1400s, people often thought that if someone was different from everyone else, it meant the person might be a witch. Joan was *very* different. Many people wondered if the voices she heard meant *she* was a witch.

Before she could go to Orléans, she had to go through a witchcraft trial. Luckily, the judges decided she was a normal girl and not a witch. She would not always be so lucky.

The Prince gave Joan a new suit of armor and her white banner decorated with lilies. Joan's voices told her about the hidden sword. When her messenger brought it back from the church, Joan was ready.

The future of France rested on the shoulders of one girl. The voices told her she could do it. Joan held her head high and set off.

Late March 1429, Poitiers

Joan rode to Orléans with an army
behind her. She brought food and supplies
for the people of the city.

Joan did not want blood shed. She told the English to save themselves and surrender. But they did not listen.

Joan had no choice. When the voices told her it was time, she raised her sword and led the army to the battlefield.

The voices promised that she would win the battle. And she did.

But she wasn't entirely happy about the victory. She cried at the sight of blood. She said she loved her banner forty times more than her sword because it could never hurt anyone.

May 4–6, 1429, Orléans

Joan still had more battles to fight. The voices warned her that she would be hurt. Joan spoke to her priest.

"Tomorrow blood will flow out of my body," she told him.

She went into the battle anyway, her banner flying high. Suddenly, an arrow hit her just below her collarbone. Joan's blood fell on the ground of Orléans.

As soon as the wound had been bandaged, Joan was back on her horse.

Joan's soldiers were proud. If a wounded girl could keep fighting, so could they.

They attacked again!

The English were shocked. And they were scared. They were so afraid that they tried to get away from Joan's army.

To escape, they had to go across a river on a bridge. But when the English soldiers crowded onto the bridge, it collapsed under them. Most of them drowned.

The city of Orléans was free!

The English still controlled much of France, though. So Joan and her army traveled over the country, fighting battle after battle. Again and again, they won.

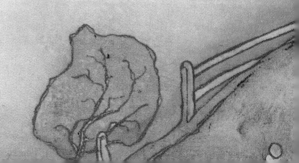

May 7–8, 1429, Orléans

Then the voices told Joan it was time for the French Prince to be crowned King.

Joan and the Prince traveled to the city of Reims (REEMZ).

Joan's family came too. She hadn't seen them since she had left home as an ordinary farmer's daughter. Now she was a war hero!

Joan watched as the Prince was crowned in a great cathedral. Thanks to Joan, he was now King!

As a reward, the new King promised that the people of Joan's village would not have to pay taxes. He kept his word. For three hundred years, long after Joan and the King had died, the people of Domrémy (dome-ray-MEE) were not taxed.

July 17, 1429, Reims

But there was no rest for Joan. The city of Compiègne (kome-PYANE) was being attacked by the Burgundians.

Joan's voices warned that she would soon be captured. Anyone else might have returned home—but not Joan!

Once more, she rode into battle.

This time, Joan and her army were outnumbered. The army retreated into Compiègne. The Burgundians were right behind them!

The Captain of Compiègne panicked. He raised the drawbridge to keep out the Burgundians.

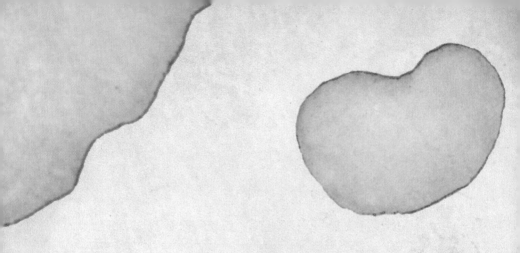

Joan was locked outside with the
enemy. She fought with everything she
had. Never had she been so brave . . .
or so alone.

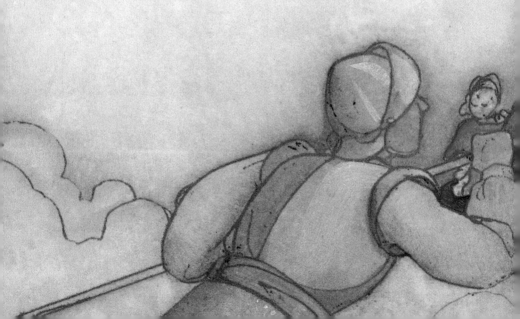

Suddenly, an enemy soldier grabbed her. He dragged her from her horse. Joan was a prisoner.

She had told the Prince that she had only a little more than a year to help France. That time was now up.

May 23, 1430, Compiègne

The Burgundians held Joan captive in
a lonely castle.

Her friends and family could not afford
to pay her ransom. The French King did
not offer. It was the English, Joan's worst
enemies, who finally bought her.

Early 1431, Rouen

The English put Joan on trial. They accused her of being a heretic—someone who did not believe in the Church. They also accused her of being a witch.

Joan wasn't allowed to have witnesses on her side, or even a lawyer. All alone, Joan answered her accusers' questions bravely.

"I am more afraid of doing wrong by saying what would displease those voices than I am of answering you," she told a surprised judge.

Joan had been tried before and found innocent. This time, she was found guilty and sentenced to be burned at the stake.

The men of the court told Joan that the
Church was abandoning her. For Joan, this
was worse than being burned alive. She
cried and did exactly what the court hoped
she would.

Even though it wasn't true, she told
them she had made up her voices.

Joan was taken back to her prison.

Had she escaped the stake?

Joan tossed and turned all night. Finally, she made a decision—a decision that would cost her life. When the priests came to see her, she told them that she could not lie: the voices were real to her.

A few days later, Joan was taken to be burned. She was tied to a stake. Someone in the crowd handed her a little wooden cross. Joan held it as the fire was lit. She was only nineteen years old.

At the end, even her captors saw her goodness. Many of them cried and turned away at the sight of the fire.

One man said he saw a dove fly out of her mouth.

"We are lost!" cried another. "We have burned a saint!"

May 30, 1431, Rouen

Joan of Arc was called many things in her lifetime. Savior. Heroine. Witch. Nearly five hundred years after she died, the Catholic Church named her a saint.

The world will never forget the farm girl from Lorraine—Saint Joan of Arc.